.CLASSICS.
Illustrated.®

Robert Louis Stevenson
THE MASTER OF BALLANTRAE

essay by
Beth Nachison, Ph.D.,
S. Connecticut State University

ACCLAIM BOOKS
STUDY GUIDE

CLASSICS Illustrated ®

The Master of Ballantrae
Originally published as Classics Illustrated no. 82

Art by Lawrence Dresser
Adaption by Ken Fitch
Cover by Enrique Alcatena

For Classics Illustrated Study Guides
computer recoloring by VanHook Studios
editor: Madeleine Robins
assistant editor: Valerie D'Orazio
design: Joseph Caponsacco

Classics Illustrated: The Master of Ballantrae © Twin Circle Publishing Co.,
a division of Frawley Enterprises; licensed to First Classics, Inc.
All new material and compilation © 1997 by Acclaim Books, Inc.

Dale-Chall R.L.: 7.3

ISBN 1-57840-049-X

Acclaim Books, New York, NY
Printed in the United States

THE STORY REALLY BEGAN WITH THE LANDING OF BONNIE PRINCE CHARLIE ON THE RUGGED NORTHERN COAST OF SCOTLAND, EARLY IN 1745...

MY LORD DURRISDEER, FATHER OF JAMES AND HENRY, WAS INCLINED TO FAVOR ENGLAND'S KING GEORGE II... WHICH WAS TO BE EXPECTED, OF COURSE. MY LORD'S TITLE AND LANDS COULD BE TAKEN BY THE CROWN. AND YET...

IF I GO WITH PRINCE CHARLIE AND HE WINS, DURRISDEER IS SAVED! AND IF HE FAILS, THEN YOU, THE ELDEST SON, HAVE BEEN FAITHFUL TO KING GEORGE. DURRISDEER IS STILL SAVED.

AND THAT IS THE TRUTH, JAMES-- ALTHOUGH I'VE NO STOMACH FOR WAR.

BAH!

BESIDES, YOU ARE THE FAVORITE! IT IS YOU WHO SHOULD STAY AT HOME WITH OUR FATHER!

YOU SPEAK LIKE ENVY, MY DEAR BROTHER! HERE, I HAVE A COIN WILL YOU LET IT DECIDE?

"I WILL STAND OR FALL BY IT," SAID MR. HENRY. "HEADS I GO; SHIELD I STAY." AND SO THE COIN WAS TOSSED AND IT FELL SHIELD-UP UPON THE FLOOR...

IT WAS THEN MISS ALISON, LORD DURRISDEER'S NIECE AND WARD, RAN TO THE GOLD PIECE, AND THERE WAS THAT QUALITY IN HER VOICE THAT WAS OF ANGER AND DESPAIR.

WE SHALL REPENT THIS, JAMES!

YOU HAVE NO HEART, JAMES! IF YOU LOVED ME AS I LOVE YOU, YOU WOULD HAVE STAYED!

WITH THAT, MISS ALISON THREW THE COIN, AND IN HER VEHEMENCE, HER AIM WAS INDEED TRUE, FOR IT CRASHED THROUGH THE STAINED GLASS WINDOW, BREAKING THE DURIE FAMILY SHIELD, WHICH MIGHT, IN A WAY, HAVE PORTENDED THE EVIL THAT WAS TO BEFALL THE HOUSE...

O! I HOPE YOU MAY BE KILLED!

THIS LOOKS LIKE A DEVIL OF A WIFE SHE WOULD BE.

AND YOU'RE A DEVIL OF A SON! SHAME TO ME THAT YOU'VE ALWAYS BEEN MY FAVORITE! NEVER HAVE I HAD FROM YOU ONE GOOD HOUR!

ALTHOUGH IT WAS IN PRETTY ILL BLOOD THAT HE DEPARTED, THE THREE SAW HIM OFF AT THE HEAD OF NEAR UPON A DOZEN MEN, PRINCIPALLY TENANTS' SONS SCRAPED TOGETHER BY FEAR OR FAVOR... THEY RODE, EACH WEARING IN HIS HAT THE WHITE COCKADE OF THE STUART HOUSE...

FAREWELL! WISH ME FORTUNE!

A SAFE RETURN! I CAN WISH NO MORE!

MR. HENRY AND MY LORD DURRIS-DEER KEPT TO THEIR AGREEMENT AND REMAINED AT HOME, SERVING HIS MAJESTY AND HAVING NO COMMERCE WITH THE MASTER. NOR DID JAMES COMMUNICATE WITH THEM. AS FOR MISS ALISON, HOWEVER, IT WAS DIFFERENT...

MY DARLING-- HOW LONG THE DAYS HAVE BEEN SINCE YOU LEFT OUR HEARTHSIDE. DO YOU FEEL THAT WAY ABOUT...

MACCONOCHIE, A SERVANT, WAS GIVEN A LETTER TO DELIVER TO THE MASTER. HE FOUND JAMES BEFORE CARLYLE, RIDING BESIDE BONNIE PRINCE CHARLIE HIMSELF.

WHAT BRINGS YOU HERE, MACCONOCHIE?

A LETTER FROM MISS ALISON, MY LORD.

WITH YOUR PERMISSION YOUR HIGHNESS...

SINCE 'TIS WRITTEN, I CAN BUT READ IT.

HE IS OF NO ACCOUNT, THE MASTER! LETTIN' THE WORDS SHE DOUBTLESS WEPT O'ER FA' SO TO THE GROUND!

So Prince Charles retreated back into Scotland, where he won a victory at Falkirk. The British, now sorely aroused, pursued the Scots to Culloden. Here on April 16, 1746, they murdered the Scots right and left and scattered them to the winds...

It was later in the year of '46, or perhaps in early '47, that MacConnochie had the misfortune to find the piece of gold that Miss Alison had tossed through the window before the Master's departure. John Paul was nearby...

I SAW YE LIFT THAT COIN, MACCONNOCHIE! AN' SO 'TIS MINE AS WELL AS YOURS!

'TIS A SORE TASK TO BITE A PIECE OF GOD IN TWA, JOHN PAUL! BUT WE WILL EACH DRINK HALF O'T AT THE CHANGE HOUSE'!

*LOCAL PUB

John Paul claimed to be uninterested in the bottle. But if he must drink to obtain his half of the gold piece, drink he would. It was when neither had much left of the coin or his wits that John Paul pointed toward the door...

LOOK, YOU! 'TIS TAM MACMORLAND! HE'LL BE BRINGIN' WORD OF THE MASTER!

John Paul staggered home as fast as his wobbly legs would take him and burst in on the family, who were at dinner...

THE MASTER IS DEAD! DEAD AT CULLODEN!

Tam Macmorland was the son of a tenant, and he lost no time in making the most of laying the blame for the Prince's defeat...

I'M HERE ALONE AND THERE'S NANE TO FOLLOW ME. AND ALL THE WHILE, WHERE WAS MY LORD HENRY? HOME AND SAFE... AND PERHAPS HOPING THE MASTER WOULD NOT RETURN!

MISS ALISON'S PRIDE WAS STUNG, FOR SHE WAS A BONE-BRED DURIE BUT HER HEART WAS TOUCHED TO SEE HER COUSIN SO UNJUSTLY USED. THAT NIGHT SHE WAS NEVER IN BED, AND THE NEXT DAY, SHE AGREED TO MARRIAGE. SO ON THE FIRST OF JUNE, 1748...

I NOW PRONOUNCE YOU MAN AND WIFE.

THEN, WHEN THE BRIDE AND GROOM WERE ALONE, MISS ALISON SAID...

I BRING YOU NO LOVE, HENRY BUT GOD KNOWS, ALL THE PITY IN THE WORLD.

PERHAPS I MAY EARN YOUR LOVE. I HAVE LOVED YOU ALWAYS.

IT WAS IN DECEMBER OF THAT YEAR OF 1748 WHEN, FRESH FROM EDINBURGH COLLEGE, I CAME TO DURRISDEER. HERETOFORE, WHAT I HAVE WRITTEN I HAVE GLEANED FROM OTHERS OVER THE YEARS. BUT FROM THIS MOMENT, MOST OF WHAT I WRITE CAME FROM OUT OF MY OWN OBSERVATION AND EXPERIENCE...

YOU ARE WELCOME, MR. MACKELLAR. I HAVE BEEN EXPECTING YOU.

THANK YOU, MY LORD.

MR. HENRY WAS A TASKMASTER ALL RIGHT, AND HE KEPT ME AT DUTIES FROM MORN TILL NIGHT. THEN ONE DAY, HE SAID...

I AM VERY PLEASED WITH YOU, MR. MACKELLAR.

I AM GLAD SIR.

BUT IT WAS EASY TO SEE THAT MR. HENRY WAS A VERY SAD MAN. IN THE COUNTING ROOM AT THE TOP OF THE HOUSE WHERE HE WORKED, HE WOULD OFTEN STAND FOR LONG TIMES, IDLY STARING OUT OF THE WINDOW...

IT WAS A SCENE OF RUGGEDNESS AND BEAUTY, WITH THE SEA ROLLING INTO THE BAY AT THE END OF THE LAND. BUT I BELIEVE MR. HENRY WAS SCARCELY AWARE OF IT...

I THOUGHT THAT THE BIRTH OF MISS KATHERINE IN THE SPRING WOULD BRIGHTEN THE HOUSEHOLD, BUT IT DIDN'T. THERE WAS ALWAYS A GHOST IN THE HOUSE--THE GHOST OF THE MASTER...

ONE CAN LITTLE REALIZE HOW I SUFFER, FATHER.

YOU MUST BE PATIENT, CHILD... HENRY'S A GOOD HUSBAND. OF COURSE, WE WERE ALL PROUD OF JAMES.

SUCH WAS THE STATE OF AFFAIRS UNTIL THE NIGHT IN APRIL 1749 WHEN THERE BEFELL THE FIRST OF A SERIES OF EVENTS THAT WERE TO BREAK SO MANY HEARTS...

THERE'S A STRANGER AT THE DOOR WILL SPEAK WITH NO ONE BUT THE CHIEF STEWARD.

VERY WELL. WITH YOUR PERMISSION MY LORDS, MY LADY.

THE NAME IS COLONEL FRANCIS BURKE. I COME ON A MISSION CONCERNING A MEMBER OF THIS FAMILY AWAY THESE MANY YEARS...

YOU... YOU MEAN THE MASTER?

AS WE SPOKE, THE OTHERS CAME TO THE DOOR...

YES, THE MASTER OF BALLANTRAE IS WELL AND NOW LIVING IN PARIS. HE SENDS YOU THESE COMPLIMENTS, SIR.

IN PARIS! ALISON...

NEVER MIND, HENRY. I SHALL NOT FAINT. I'M QUITE WELL.

THE EFFECT ON MRS. DURIE IS QUITE NATURAL, COLONEL BURKE. WE WERE ALL BROUGHT UP LIKE BROTHER AND SISTER.

THEN COLONEL BURKE GAVE AN ACCOUNT OF THE ACTIVITIES OF THE MASTER OF BALLANTRAE DURING THE YEARS WE HAD THOUGHT HIM DEAD. BURKE HAD ESCAPED AFTER THE DEFEAT AT CULLODEN AND WAS HIDING OUT. ONE DAY...

EH? IT IS YOU, LORD DURRISDEER! I THOUGHT YOU WERE KILLED IN THE BATTLE!

AS YOU CAN SEE, COLONEL, BURKE, I'VE DISAPPOINTED YOU!

I COULD SAY YOU SPEAK THE TRUTH, JAMES DURIE. FOR I SWEAR THAT YOU COAXED THE PRINCE TO HIS DEFEAT BY AGREEING WITH HIM FOR NO BETTER PURPOSE THAN TO BETTER YOUR OWN END.

YOU'LL FIND, IF YOU TRY TO SETTLE WITH ME, THAT I'LL BETTER MY OWN ENDS WITH THE SWORD ALSO.

THEN LET'S GET AT IT AND FINISH THIS THING ONCE AND FOR ALL.

WAIT! THERE'S PLENTY OF TIME TO SLASH ONE ANOTHER TO RIBBONS.

LET THE TOSS DECIDE. HEADS WE'LL REMAIN FRIENDS AND AID EACH OTHER IN ESCAPING THE KING'S MEN; SHIELD WE'LL FIGHT IT TO A FINISH.

MAN, I'LL AGREE TO THAT. IT TOUCHES MY ROMANTIC FANCY.

THE COIN WAS TOSSED AND HEADS CAME UP...

SO THE MASTER AND COLONEL BURKE MADE WAY IN PEACE TOWARD A LOCH* WHERE THEY FOUND A SHIP AT ANCHOR STATIONED THERE, THE MASTER HAD LEARNED, TO INSURE THE ESCAPE OF PRINCE CHARLES AND HIS MEN IN THE EVENT OF DEFEAT...

*LAKE

AHOY, THERE! AHOY!

AHOY!

At a time like that, a man of piety, such as Colonel Burke, appears in his true light, for he kept to his devotions. As for the master, he was scarcely moved. The worse the storm grew, the more he delighted in taunting Burke...

HO-HO, MY DEAR COLONEL BURKE! DO YOU BELIEVE YOUR MISERABLE LITTLE PRAYERS WILL GET PAST THE HOWLING OF THAT WIND?

On the fourth day, the wind fell, leaving the ship dismasted and heaving on the billows... and for five days, it drifted aimlessly.

And then...

SAIL TO STAR-BOARD!

WE'RE SAVED!

I WOULDN'T CROW UNTIL I HAD A CLOSER VIEW OF OUR RESCUERS, CAPTAIN.

And indeed the master had shown his keen perception, for the crew that set out to come to the rescue of the stricken ship was a rough-looking lot and the appearance of the skipper of the ship more terrible than all the rest.. in one...

PULL! PULL, YOU THICK-SKULLED, DRUNKEN FOOLS!

WHERE'S THE SKIPPER OF THIS ROTTING HULK?

THE KING'S SHIP OPENED FIRE FIRST...

NEVER IN ITS LIFE HAD THAT DRUNKEN CREW SOBERED SO FAST! TEACH, FIRST TO RUN FOR COVER, SHUT HIMSELF IN HIS CABIN. IT WAS ONLY THE CLOAK OF NIGHT THAT DELIVERED THEM FROM DISASTER, AND THE NEXT MORNING, THE MASTER FACED THE CAPTAIN WHEN HE SHOWED HIMSELF...

GET BACK INSIDE, YOU SNIVELING COWARD! WE SAW NOTHING OF YOU YESTERDAY, WHEN YOU WERE NEEDED!

AT THE WORD FROM BALLANTRAE, BURKE AND TWO OTHERS SPRANG FROM THE FLOOR...

IVE BEEN DONE A-FOUL! I'LL GET REVENGE!

YOUR NAME, PERHAPS, SHOULD BE CAPTAIN *LEARN*, NOT CAPTAIN *TEACH*!

THESE TWO OTHERS WERE GRADY AND DUTTON. TWO MEMBERS OF THE "SAINTE MARIE DES ANGES," TAKEN WITH BURKE AND THE MASTER...

HURRY NOW OR WE SHALL BE TOO LATE!

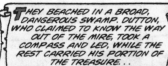

THEY BEACHED IN A BROAD, DANGEROUS SWAMP. DUTTON, WHO CLAIMED TO KNOW THE WAY OUT OF THE MIRE, TOOK A COMPASS AND LED, WHILE THE REST CARRIED HIS PORTION OF THE TREASURE...

BUT BEFORE THEY HAD GONE FAR, GRADY, WHO HAD LAGGED BEHIND, SUDDENLY STUMBLED AND...

HELP!! HELP! I'M... I'M DROWNING!

TOO BAD-- THAT GRADY HAD TO TAKE HIS TREASURE DOWN WITH HIM. IT WOULD HAVE SPLIT THREE WAYS QUITE HANDSOMELY.

IT WAS AT THAT TIME THE REMAINING THREE DECIDED TO DETERMINE THE EXACT DISTANCE TO THE RISING LAND BEYOND THE SWAMP. DUTTON AND BURKE CLIMBED A NEARBY TREE RISING OUT OF THE SOGGY GROUND... FOR THE FOG WAS CLEARING FAST...

LOOK YONDER! IT'S BUT AN HOUR'S WALK TO RISING GROUND! WE'LL SOON BE OUT OF THIS MIRE!

SO EAGER WAS DUTTON TO GET TO HIGH GROUND THAT HE SET OFF CARELESSLY. SUDDENLY, HE TURNED IN TERROR TO THE OTHERS...

LEND A HAND, DURIE! I'M IN A BAD PLACE!

OH, I DON'T KNOW! YOUR TREASURE SPLIT TWO WAYS IS EVEN BETTER!

HELP ME OR DIE AND THE DEVIL WITH YOU!

PUT DOWN YOUR GUN, DUTTON. I WAS MERELY JOKING!

SET DOWN YOUR GUN AND GIVE ME YOUR HANDS.

VERY WELL, BUT GET ME QUICK!

DUTTON WAS SLOW OF THOUGHT AND, FOLLOWING THE MASTER'S DIRECTION, DUTIFULLY LAID HIS GUN UPON THE MUD. WHEREUPON THE MASTER MOVED WITH LIGHTNING SPEED.

THE FOG HAD QUITE CLEARED AND THAT IS WHAT STOPPED THE PROTEST ON THE LIPS OF BURKE AGAINST THE FOUL TREACHERY SHOWN BY THE MASTER. FOR A KING'S SHIP SHOWED ON THE WATER AND A SMALL BOAT BEARING KING'S MEN WAS HEADING TOWARD THE "SARAH"...

IT APPEARS OUR ESCAPE WAS WELL TIMED. BUT LET'S BE ON, COLONEL BURKE. THE FARTHER FROM THIS LOCATION THE BETTER!

THE FUGITIVES MADE ALL HASTE AWAY FROM THE SCENE. SOME HOURS LATER, THEY CLIMBED A DUNE WHICH GAVE THEM A VIEW OF A TRADING VESSEL AND CREW...

WE'RE NOT INLAND AT ALL, COLONEL BURKE. IF WE DON'T CONVINCE THAT CAPTAIN YONDER TO TAKE US ABOARD, I FEAR WE SHALL BE HIDING A LONG WHILE IN THIS COUNTRYSIDE!

BOARDING THE TRADING SHIP, THEY ARRIVED IN DUE TIME IN AMERICA. FROM THERE, THEY SAILED UP THE HUDSON RIVER TO A SETTLEMENT KNOWN AS ALBANY, NEW YORK...

IT WAS THEIR INTENTION TO REACH A FRENCH FORT ON A CERTAIN LAKE CHAMPLAIN. TO ACCOMPLISH THIS JOURNEY, THEY WERE FORTUNATE IN HIRING A GUIDE OF GREAT ABILITY AND KNOWLEDGE OF THE ADIRONDACK MOUNTAIN COUNTRY...

THE GUIDE'S NAME WAS CHEW. THE JOURNEY THROUGH THE WILDERNESS WAS MADE CONSIDERABLY LIGHTER BY HIS KNOWLEDGE. NEVERTHELESS, IT WAS AN AWFUL ORDEAL...

LET'S CAMP HERE. I CAN'T GO ANOTHER STEP!

BEFORE THE JOURNEY WAS HALF-COMPLETED, CHEW BECAME SERIOUSLY ILL...

CHEW'S GOING TO DIE, BURKE. OH, WELL, HE WAS TOO CURIOUS ABOUT WHENCE WE CAME AND WHAT WE CARRIED WITH US. WE'LL MANAGE WITHOUT HIM!

THEY LEFT CHEW ASLEEP IN A SHALLOW GRAVE AND CONTINUED, STUMBLING, FALLING, AND BOSS-ING TO THE KNEES. THEN DURING A PORTAGE ON THE THIRD DAY...

LOOK OUT, YOU FOOL!

*CARRY OVERLAND

LET THIS BE AN END TO IT! YOU GO YOUR WAY AND I'LL GO MINE!

THAT WILL BE MUCH TO MY LIKING!

IT WAS AN ABRUPT SEPARATION. WHEN THEY WERE APART A LONG TIME, THE MASTER SET ABOUT TO BURY HIS SHARE OF THE TREASURE...

THE MASTER AND COLONEL BURKE WOULD HAVE PERISHED IN THE WILDERNESS, HAD NOT PARTIES FROM FORT ST. FREDERICK PICKED THEM UP. BURKE WAS FIRST TO BE RESCUED. ON THE MASTER'S LATER ARRIVAL, THE COLONEL GREETED THE OTHER LIKE A BROTHER...

JAMES, MY FRIEND! I THOUGHT YOU WERE LOST TO ME FOREVER!

AFTER THE MASTER TOLD BURKE OF HIS BEING PENNILESS, BURKE INSISTED ON PAYING BALLANTRAE'S PASSAGE TO FRANCE... AND SO BURKE CAME TO THE CLOSE OF HIS STORY...

AND THERE HE IS, AS HIS LETTER WILL EXPLAIN!

YES... YES, I FIND IT'S AS YOU SAY, COLONEL BURKE. JAMES IS ALIVE... AND WELL...

HENRY THEN ABRUPTLY FOLDED THE LETTER AND STARTED FROM THE ROOM, SAYING...

COME, MACKELLAR, WE HAVE SOME BUSINESS.

YOUR PERMISSION, MY LADY, MY LORD...

MR. HENRY LED ME DIRECTLY TO THE COUNTING ROOM. HE BEGAN AT ONCE COUNTING OUT A SUM OF MONEY, AND SAYING HALF ALOUD...

IT'S HIS! EVERYTHING! WHILE I CAN'T PAY ALL HE ASKS, THE SUM WILL BE MORE THAN HE EXPECTS!

BUT, MR. HENRY, YOU CANNOT AFFORD TO SEND SO LARGE A SUM, EVEN TO A BROTHER! THERE IS THE MORTGAGE!

IN THAT LETTER, HE CALLS ME A NIGGARDLY DOG, MACKELLAR! MORTGAGE OR NO, I SHALL PAY HIM OFF, EVEN IF I RUIN THE ESTATE AND GO BAREFOOT!

THE REMITTANCE TO THE MASTER MADE A DEEP HOLE IN THE ESTATE. THREE WEEKS LATER, I WENT TO EDINBURGH TO SEEK FINANCING...

BUT THAT'S USURY, I TELL YOU! ASKING THE RATE YOU DO FOR A MORTGAGE!

IT'S MORE THAN I SHOULD LOAN YOU. IF YOU DON'T WANT THAT RATE, I'LL PLACE MY MONEY ELSEWHERE.

FOR SEVEN YEARS, THE BLOODSUCKER IN PARIS DRAINED THE ESTATE. MR. HENRY PINCHED MONEY EVEN TIGHTER TO SEND IT TO HIM. BUT THERE CAME A BREAKING POINT...

AND NOW YOU DENY OUR ANNUAL TRIP TO EDINBURGH! YOU ARE SELFISH, HENRY!

WE CAN'T AFFORD THE TRIP! WE SHAN'T GO!

WITH THAT, THEY BOTH RETIRED TO THEIR ROOMS. I HAD BEEN CONSCIENTIOUS TO KEEP ALL TO MYSELF THAT WITH WHICH I HAD BEEN ENTRUSTED. BUT THAT NIGHT, I DECIDED TO SPEAK...

WHY DO YOU ASK TO SEE ME AT THIS HOUR, MR. MACKELLAR?

I MUST SPEAK OF IMPORTANT MATTERS, MY LADY. AND I MUST SPEAK PRIVATELY!

MRS. HENRY SPOKE TO MR. HENRY. AND THEREAFTER, NO MORE MONEY WENT TO THE MASTER AND THERE WAS BETTER FEELING BETWEEN THE TWO. I TOOK TO WALKING NEAR THE EDGES OF THE ESTATE, BESIDE THE BAY...

I CAN'T BEAR HEARING YOU CALL MR. HENRY SELFISH AND KEEP QUIET. MR. HENRY, IN THE PAST SEVEN YEARS, HAS SENT HIS BROTHER OVER EIGHT THOUSAND POUNDS!

MR. MACKELLAR! THERE'S NOT THAT MUCH TO BE HAD FROM THE ESTATE! YOU'VE DONE WELL TO TELL ME THIS!

I LEARNED THE HABITS OF THE FREEHOLDERS* WHO FREQUENTED THE SHORE. ONE EVENING I KNEW FROM THEIR SIGNAL FIRES SOMETHING WAS UP...

HEAD STRAIGHT IN, CAPTAIN CRAIL.

*SMUGGLERS

THAT, THEN, IS THE WAY THINGS WENT. SURLY WAS THE MASTER WHEN ALONE WITH HENRY AND ME, CHARMING WHEN OTHERS WERE ABOUT. MOREOVER, HE QUITE ENCHANTED MRS. HENRY, AND WAS SEEN OFTEN WITH HER AND LITTLE KATHERINE IN THE GARDEN...

IT WAS IN NOVEMBER OF 1756 THAT THE MASTER ARRIVED, AND NOW IT WAS LATE IN FEBRUARY, 1757. THINGS BETWEEN HENRY AND BALLANTRAE GREW STEADILY WORSE. ONE NIGHT, THE 27TH. OF FEBRUARY, THE THREE OF US PLAYED CARDS UNTIL AFTER MIDNIGHT, MRS. HENRY AND MY LORD DURRISDEER HAVING LONG SINCE RETIRED...

HENRY, YOU'RE A BUMPKIN! YOU BORE ME TO TEARS! HOW CAN I STAND LIVING WITH YOU?

YOU MAY LEAVE AT ANY MOMENT.

AND WHAT WOULD ALISON DO? YOU KNOW I COULD WIN HER FROM YOU WITHOUT TRYING! SHOULD I LET HER ROT AWAY IN YOUR STUFFY PRESENCE?

ENOUGH!

YOU COWARD!

I MUST HAVE BLOOD! I MUST HAVE BLOOD FOR THIS!

PRAY GOD IT SHALL BE YOURS!

MACKELLAR SHALL SEE US DUEL FAIR! I THINK THAT IS NECESSARY!

O, NO! NO, NO, GENTLEMEN! SHAME ON YOU BOTH!

THE BROTHERS, HOWEVER, WERE MUCH TOO DETERMINED TO HAVE THEIR DIFFERENCES SETTLED BY ME. TREMBLING, I ADMIT, IN COWARDLY FEAR, I HELD THE TWO CANDLES AND WATCHED THE SALUTE THAT FENCERS GIVE...

THE DUEL WAS FAST AND FURIOUS, FILLED WITH HAIRBREADTH ACTION THAT LEFT ME IN CONSTANT ANXIETY AND TENSION...

I'M NO JUDGE OF DUELING, BUT IT SEEMS MR. HENRY HAD THE UPPER HAND FROM THE START, CROWDING IN UPON HIS FOE WITH A CONTAINED AND GLOWING FURY...

THE MASTER NOW RECOGNIZED HIMSELF FOR LOST, AND IT BROUGHT HIM TO USE A FOUL BLOW. HE HELD MR. HENRY'S SWORD AND THRUST WITH HIS OWN. MR. HENRY TURNED AGILELY...

.. AND WITH A THRUST AS FAST AS LIGHTNING, MR. HENRY SENT HIS SWORD THROUGH THE MASTER'S BODY!

DEAD?... DEAD?

GOD FORGIVE US, MR. HENRY! HE IS DEAD!

I GOT MR. HENRY TO ENTER THE HOUSE, BUT HE WAS A LOST MAN...

WHAT HAVE I DONE? WHO IS TO TELL FATHER?

IT WAS A DUTY THAT FELL ON MY SHOULDER, AND I CALLED FIRST TO AWAKEN MRS. HENRY. I TOLD HER, WITH GREAT FEELING, HOW HER HUSBAND HAD STRUCK IN HER DEFENSE, AND PLEADED THAT SHE COMFORT HIM. THEN TO THE OLD LORD, WHO WAS A LONG WHILE IN THE UNDERSTANDING...

OH, 'TIS A PITY! AND I'M PART TO BLAME! WE MUST COVER THIS THING IN A WAY THAT SHALL NOT BRING SHAME UPON OUR HOUSE!

ON DESCENDING THE STAIRS, I SAW THAT MRS. HENRY COULD MAKE NO IMPRESSION ON HER HUSBAND, BUT AS SOON AS HE SAW THE OLD LORD...

O, FATHER, FATHER, WHAT HAVE I DONE? AND WE WERE BAIRNS TOGETHER!

AND THEN IT WAS HE SAW MRS. HENRY, AS IF FOR THE FIRST TIME...

AND, ALISON, TRY TO FORGIVE ME, TOO! NOT AS YOUR HUSBAND, BUT AS THE BAIRN WHO ONCE PLAYED WITH YOU AND WITH JAMES!

THERE HAD BEEN A SOUND AS OF ROWING, COMING O'ER THE STILL NIGHT AIR...

WE MUST PUT THEM OUT! AND LET NO ONE, NOT EVEN THE SERVANTS, KNOW OF THIS AWFUL THING TONIGHT! WE MUST BURY MY SON! EVEN AT ONCE!

SHH! LISTEN! MEN IN A BOAT UPON THE BAY! AND THE CANDLES LIGHTED OUTSIDE!

BUT LOOK! THE BODY IS GONE! IT WAS THERE IN THAT POOL OF BLOOD! COULD IT BE...

THOSE MEN--FREE-TRADERS, NO DOUBT--HAVE TAKEN MY SON OFF EVEN WHILE WE SPAKE! PERHAPS THEN HE IS NOT DEAD! WE WILL LET IT BE KNOWN THUS! WE WILL SAY THAT HE LEFT IN THE NIGHT!

THE WIND HAD SPRUNG UP AND EVEN WHILE WE STOOD UNCERTAINLY, SNOW SHIPPED AGAINST US.

THE SNOW IS A BLESSING-IT WILL COVER ALL! TAKE THE SWORD, MR. MACKELLAR, AND WIPE IT CLEAN. THEN LET US GO INSIDE, FOR WE CAN DO NO MORE HERE!

MY LORD! THE MASTER'S HEART WAS STOPPED! I LISTENED! I FELT! I DO NOT UNDER-STAND!

WHEN THE MEMBERS OF THE FAMILY HAD RETIRED, IT WAS MY DUTY TO INSPECT THE MASTER'S ROOM TO REMOVE EVIDENCE OF HIS PRESENCE. THERE I FOUND HIS BAGS ALMOST ALL PACKED! THE MASTER, THEN, HAD PLANNED TO LEAVE TONIGHT, SECRETLY! DOUBTLESS WITH THE MEN WHO TOOK HIM OFF!

CONCEALING THE MASTER'S LUGGAGE IN AN UNUSED ROOM, I ADMIT I DIPPED A LITTLE INTO ONE OF THE PORTMANTEAUX. WHAT I FOUND LEFT ME STARTLED...

THESE LETTERS INDICATE THE MASTER WAS REALLY SERVING HIS MAJESTY WHILE CLAIMING TO SERVE PRINCE CHARLIE. ALSO, HOW HE DRAINED THE ESTATE OF FUNDS. HMMM! IT'S A WEAPON I SHALL USE IF HE EVER RETURNS TO THIS HOUSE!

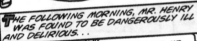

THE FOLLOWING MORNING, MR. HENRY WAS FOUND TO BE DANGEROUSLY ILL AND DELIRIOUS...

OH.. DON'T LET JAMIE DROWN! DON'T LET JAMIE DROWN!

QUICK, HOLD HIM, MR. MACKELLAR! HE HAS GONE BACK TO HIS BOYHOOD! I REMEMBER THE INCIDENT!

FOR WEEKS, MR. HENRY HOVERED BETWEEN LIFE AND DEATH. THEN, ONE DAY, HIS EYES OPENED WITH SOME LIGHT OF INTELLIGENCE. HE LOOKED AT MRS. HENRY WITHOUT RECOGNITION, HOWEVER, AND THEN TURNED TO ME...

MACKELLAR! MY OLD FRIEND!

OH, MR. HENRY! YOU RECOGNIZED ME!

I KNEW MRS. HENRY WAS HURT BY MR. HENRY'S DISINTEREST IN HER DURING THAT SANE MOMENT. I SET ABOUT ARRANGING THE PAPERS I HAD FOUND WITH THE MASTER'S THINGS... A RECORD THAT WOULD SHOW THE MASTER IN HIS TRUE LIGHT...

WHEN YOU READ THESE, MY LADY, YOU'LL KNOW UNDER WHAT STRAIN MR. HENRY HAS LIVED THESE MANY YEARS. YOU WILL BE MORE TOLERANT OF HIM.

NEXT MORNING, I CALLED ON MRS. HENRY. I EXPECTED I KNOW NOT WHAT, BUT CERTAINLY NOT THE ACTION SHE HAD TAKEN...

MY LADY! YOU'VE BURNED THE RECORDS OF THE MASTER'S DEEDS. I'D THOUGHT TO USE THEM AS A WEAPON AGAINST HIM SHOULD HE RETURN!

JAMES HAS NO SHAME, HE WOULD USE THOSE VERY LETTERS TO DISGRACE THE HOUSE. THE NAME OF DURIE IS TOO SACRED TO BE DRAGGED THROUGH THE MIRE FOR REVENGE!

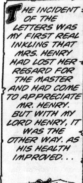

THE INCIDENT OF THE LETTERS WAS MY FIRST REAL INKLING THAT MRS. HENRY HAD LOST HER REGARD FOR THE MASTER AND HAD COME TO APPRECIATE MR. HENRY. BUT WITH MY LORD HENRY, IT WAS THE OTHER WAY. AS HIS HEALTH IMPROVED...

HENRY, IS THERE SOMETHING I CAN DO FOR YOU? MAY I BRING YOU SOME...

MACKELLAR, LET US WALK A BIT IN THE GARDEN. THERE ARE THINGS I WOULD LIKE TO SEE.

THAT DAY, I FIRST SUSPECTED THAT MR. HENRY, PERHAPS, HAD NOT HIS FULL SENSES. REACHING THE GARDEN, MR. HENRY SAID...

SHOW ME WHERE YOU BURIED HIM!

BURIED? YOU MEAN THE MASTER? IN ALL PROBABILITY, YOU DID NOT KILL HIM, MR. HENRY. I BELIEVE HE IS STILL ALIVE!

MR. HENRY TURNED FROM HIS WIFE AS IF SHE HAD NOT SPOKEN. I SAW HER STIFLE A SOB OF ANGUISH AT MR. HENRY'S ABRUPT DISMISSAL OF HER.

NOTHING CAN KILL THAT MAN, MACKELLAR! NOTHING! HE'LL HAUNT ME TILL I DIE!

MR. HENRY!

AS TIME WENT ON, EXCEPT FOR REFERENCES TO THE MASTER, MR. HENRY BECAME ALMOST TOO CONTENT WITH LIFE. LORD DURRISDEER SOON FALTERED AND DIED. THEN, IN ____ JULY, BESIDE HIMSELF WITH JOY...

MY SON! MY VERY OWN! A SON TO INHERIT THE ESTATE, TO CARRY ____ ON THE NAME!

THE CHILD, NAMED ALEXANDER, WAS THE LIGHT OF MR. HENRY'S LIFE, AND AS THE BOY GREW OLDER, MR. HENRY SEEMED TO GROW YOUNGER, AS IF TRYING TO MEET ALEXANDER ON COMMON GROUND...

FATHER, I'M TIRED! I DON'T WANT TO SEARCH FOR ANY MORE CHESTNUTS!

COME THEN, DEAR BOY, I SHALL CARRY YOU HOME.

MR. HENRY, I WAS COMING TO SEEK YOU. MRS. HENRY FEARED LEST YOU TAKE COLD.

COLD! BAH! MR. MACKELLAR, DO YOU KNOW I AM NOW A VERY HAPPY MAN?

THE MASTER HAD NOW BEEN GONE SEVEN YEARS, AND I HAD HOPES WE WOULD NOT HEAR FROM HIM AGAIN. BUT EVEN THEN, FINAL TRAGEDIES WERE IN THE MAKING.

THERE'S BUT ONE INCIDENT IN THE LIFE OF THE MASTER IN HIS WANDERINGS ABROAD THAT I CAN REPORT FROM THE NOTES SENT ME BY COLONEL BURKE. IT SEEMS THAT BURKE HAD JOURNEYED INTO INDIA AS A SOLDIER OF FORTUNE. THERE, ON A NIGHT WHEN CELEBRATING LIBERTY WITHOUT LEAVE...

LOOK YONDER! OUR COMMANDANT! IF HE SEES US HERE, MY FRIEND, IT'LL MEAN TROUBLE! COME! OVER THE WALL!

BOTH BURKE AND HIS COMPANION WERE SAFE FROM DETECTION, BUT AS THEY LAY INSIDE THE GARDEN WHERE THEY WERE HIDING...

LOOK, BURKE! A LIGHT IN THE WINDOW THERE! IF THEY LOOK FRIENDLY, PERHAPS WE MAY FIND SOME FOOD AND A BED TO REST.

BEDAD! AND COME TO THINK OF IT, I'M HUNGRY. SO LET'S SEE WHAT WE CAN SEE!

THE OTHER, AN INDIAN, ANSWERED IN HIS NATIVE TONGUE...

SAHIB UNDERSTANDS NO ENGLISH, BUT HE THINKS YOU BETTER GO AWAY!

THE DEVIL FETCH HIM! TELL THE SAHIB I CONSIDER HIM NO GENTLEMAN!

THEY APPROACHED CAUTIOUSLY AT FIRST, AND THEN AS THEY DREW NEAR, BURKE UTTERED AN EXCLAMATION OF SURPRISE...

BALLANTRAE! BE-DAD, I'M GLAD IT'S YOU! WE ARE INDEED FAMISHED FOR FOOD!

I MENTION THAT ONE INCIDENT BECAUSE IT IS CONNECTED WITH EVENTS THAT WERE TO CHANGE MY WHOLE LIFE AND THAT OF MY PATRONS. WHAT THE MASTER WAS DOING IN INDIA, I DO NOT KNOW. BUT THERE WAS A MORNING IN APRIL, 1764, WHEN I WAS LATE IN RISING. I HURRIED DOWN STAIRS...

IS SOMETHING GONE WRONG? I HAVE A STRANGE PREMONITION OF EVIL THAT I CANNOT SHAKE!

HA! SO IT IS YOU!

EVEN MYSELF WORTHY MACKELLAR! AND THIS IS A NATIVE GENTLEMAN OF INDIA, SECUNDRA DASS.

I HAD THOUGHT TO GO AT ONCE TO MR. HENRY, BUT FOUND HIM THERE BEHIND ME. "WE MUST SEE TO BREAKFAST FOR THREE TRAVELERS."

PLEASE DO, HENRY. I'M AS HUNGRY AS A HAWK SINCE JOHN PAUL ADMITTED ME!

IF YOU STAY HERE, YOU'LL ADDRESS ME AS LORD DURRISDEER!

THEN MR. HENRY TURNED, BIDDING ME TO FOLLOW HIM. HE WENT AT ONCE TO THE ROOM OF JOHN PAUL AND ENTERED WITHOUT SUMMONS. JOHN PAUL WAS, OR FEIGNED TO BE, ASLEEP. BUT MR. HENRY SPOKE DIRECTLY TO HIM, AND IT WOKE HIM UP SOON ENOUGH...

JOHN PAUL, YOU'VE ADMITTED MY BROTHER AGAINST MY ORDERS! NOW UP AND BEGONE--EVEN AFTER THESE MANY YEARS!

I THEN SUGGESTED TAKING NEWS TO MRS. HENRY, WITH WHICH MR. HENRY WAS AGREEABLE...

AS YOU KNOW MACKELLAR, I HAVE MONEY AND PROPERTY OF MY OWN IN AMERICA. WE SHALL PACK AND LEAVE THE HOUSE SECRETLY THIS VERY NIGHT!

GIVE HIM BED AND BOARD, MY LADY, AND LEAVE MACKELLAR TO HOUND HIM OTHERWISE. I SHALL WATCH THE VALUES HERE LIKE A DOG AT HIS HEELS, SO THAT HE GETS NO MORE!

IT WAS ALL DONE IN GREATEST SECRECY. THAT NIGHT, THE MASTER RETIRED WITHOUT SUSPICION AND THE FAMILY AT ONCE, THEREAFTER, TOOK TO A WAITING CARRIAGE...

I'M NOT HAPPY ABOUT THIS, MACKELLAR. I WOULDN'T HAVE IT SAID I'M RUNNING AWAY FROM JAMES!

YOU HAVE YOUR WIFE AND CHILDREN TO THINK OF, MY LORD.

WE WAVED THEM GOODBYE. MY HEART WAS HEAVY, YET GREATLY RELIEVED. MR. HENRY HAD ESCAPED THE TALONS OF THE "BIRD OF PREY" ONCE MORE NESTED IN DURRISDEER; LEGALLY, I HAD BEEN MADE THE KEEPER OF ALL DURRISDEER. I WOULD NOT GIVE WAY TO THE MASTER OF BALLANTRAE...

I HAD THE MASTER CALLED AT THE CUSTOMARY EARLY HOUR AND AWAITED HIS COMING WITH A QUIET MIND...

WE'RE A SMALL PARTY, MACKELLAR! HOW COMES THAT?

YOU'LL GROW ACCUSTOMED TO IT. YOU AND I, AND YOUR FRIEND, MR. DASS, ARE ALL WHO ARE LEFT. THE REST HAVE DEPARTED. WHERE, YOU'LL NEVER LEARN.

AND FOR MONEY?

FOOD AND LODGING YOU MAY HAVE. AS FOR MONEY, I HAVE NO ORDERS.

YOU SHALL SEE ME SPLIT THIS HOUSE IN TWO! WITHIN A WEEK, I SHALL KNOW THE WHEREABOUTS OF MY TIMID BROTHER, WHO RUNS FROM ME IN FEAR!

THEREAFTER, THE MASTER QUITE WON ME OVER WITH HIS CHARM. HE SPOKE NO MORE ABOUT MR. HENRY. HIS FRIENDLY MANNER SOOTHED MY VANITY...

ARE YOU NOT LEAVING ON SOME MERRIMENT THIS NIGHT, MR. JAMES?

NO, I SHALL STAY HOME. PULL UP A CHAIR, MY FRIEND, AND WE SHALL ENJOY A GLASS OF WINE TOGETHER.

AS FOR SECUNDRA DASS, HE WAS CONTINUALLY TRAVELING TO AND FRO IN THE HOUSE, TURNING UP WHERE YOU LEAST EXPECTED HIM...

I WONDER WELL HOW MR. HENRY AND HIS LADY WILL FARE IN NEW YORK?

SH-H-H! LOOK YOU! FROM AROUND THE CORNER!

THE MAN IS LIKE A GHOST, I SWEAR IT!

A BOON TO US THAT HE UNDERSTANDS NO ENGLISH!

IT WAS ALMOST THREE WEEKS SINCE MR. HENRY HAD LEFT. ONE MORNING, THE MASTER STRETCHED LAZILY AND SAID CHEERFULLY, "WELL, I THINK WE SHOULD SOON BE PACKING." "ARE YOU LEAVING?" I ASKED. "YES, FOR NEW YORK." HE ANSWERED.

NEW YORK!

INDEED! WILL YOU COME ALONG? YOU'LL NEED TO PAY YOUR OWN PASSAGE. I'VE ENOUGH FOR SECUNDRA DASS AND ME, BUT, I FEAR, NOT FOR YOU!

I SAID IT WOULD BE A WEEK AND IT HAS TAKEN ME THREE TO FIND OUT. BUT HOW WILL YOU DO, MACKELLAR--STAY OR GO?

I GO WITH YOU.

WE FOUND A SHIP IN GLASGOW THAT WAS ABOUT TO SAIL. IT WAS CALLED THE "NONESUCH," AND AN APPROPRIATE NAME IT WAS. SHE WAS A VERY OLD VESSEL. FOR A WEEK, HOWEVER, WE HAD CLEAR SAILING AND GOOD WIND...

THE MASTER HIMSELF WAS MOST GENIAL, WHICH IS MORE THAN I CAN SAY FOR MYSELF. WHEN MY PATIENCE WOULD STAND NO MORE CIVILITY AND I TURNED ANGRILY UPON HIM, HE WOULD GO OFF BY HIMSELF AND READ...

THEN FOLLOWED FOUL WEATHER, LIKE TO SINK THE SHIP. I SAW IN IT, AT FIRST, A RAY OF COMFORT. IF THE SHIP FLOUNDERED, WE WOULD GO DOWN, AND MR. HENRY AND HIS FAMILY WOULD BE SAVED THIS LAST INDIGNITY...

THE THOUGHT BECAME AN OBSESSION. IF I COULD BRING ABOUT THE MASTER'S DEATH, THAT, TOO, WOULD PREVENT HIS REACHING NEW YORK...

AHA, MACKELLAR! THAT WAS A GOOD TRY, BUT NOT GOOD ENOUGH! BUT I MUST SAY, I THINK MORE OF YOU TO KNOW YOU HAVE BLOOD IN YOUR VEINS!

I WILL BE PLAIN. ALL THESE GENTLEMEN HERE, INCLUDING HIS HONOR, GOVERNOR CLINTON, KNOW WELL OF YOUR INFAMY. YOU MAY STAY... AND I SHALL SEE YOU OBTAIN JUST ENOUGH TO KEEP YOU DECENTLY ALIVE...

I TAKE IT WITHOUT SHAME, FOR I CONSIDER IT MINE ALREADY.

THE CONDITION IS YOU SPEAK TO NO MEMBER OF MY FAMILY EXCEPT MYSELF.

THE MASTER CHOSE A POOR SECTION OF THE SETTLEMENT FOR HIS RESIDENCE, AND PROMPTLY SET UP A SHOP WITH A SIGN PLAINLY DESIGNED TO DEGRADE THE DURIE NAME AND TO ADVERTISE MR. HENRY AS A VILLAIN...

JAMES DURIE FORMERLY MASTER OF BALLANTRAE CLOTHES NEATLY CLOUTED*

SECUNDRA DASS DECAYED° GENTLEMAN OF INDIA FINE GOLDSMITH WORK

*MENDED

°REDUCED TO POVERTY

MATTERS IN THE HOUSEHOLD INDEED APPEARED TO BE IN A HAPPIER STATE THAN I HAD IMAGINED WOULD EVER COME TO PASS...

I BLESS HEAVEN, MR. MACKELLAR, THAT MY FATHER SHOULD HAVE LEFT ME A PARADISE SUCH AS THIS!

I'M MORE THAN HAPPY FOR YOU, MY LADY!

THERE WAS A STRANGE LIGHT IN MR. HENRY'S EYES AND HE SEEMED TO BE RELISHING A CERTAIN INWARD SECRET JOY THAT SEEMED TO ME NOT QUITE WHOLESOME. EACH MORNING HE WALKED OUT FROM THE HOUSE, AND HIS JOURNEY GAVE ME MUCH CONCERN...

MR. HENRY'S FEET SEEMED SO TO TREAD IN A DEFINITE DIRECTION THAT I COULD NOT THINK BUT THAT HE WAS ON SOME ERRANT MISCHIEF, AND I TOOK THE LIBERTY TO FOLLOW HIM ON A CERTAIN DAY...

HAS MY LORD A SECRET LOVER WHOM HE MUST MEET THAT HE HURRIES SO?

I VIEWED MR. HENRY FROM AFAR AND SAW, TO MY HORROR, THAT HE HAD COME TO STARE WITH A CERTAIN GRINNING RELISH AT THE MASTER IN HIS STATE OF POVERTY. I GASPED, FOR I REALIZED IT WAS HATE, NOT LOVE, THAT BROUGHT HIM OUT EACH DAY WITH A REGULARITY THAT HAD BECOME RITUAL...

WHEN MR. HENRY WALKED BACK, I WAITED UNTIL HE WAS NEAR ME AND RAN TO HIM...

MR. HENRY, FORGIVE ME, BUT I'VE SEEN YOU STANDING BEFORE THE MASTER! YOU'RE NURTURING HATE, AND IT'S NO MANNER OF BEHAVIOR!

I GROW FAT UPON IT!

AND ANOTHER DAY A WEEK OR SO LATER, I CONTRIVED TO COME UPON THE BROTHERS AT THEIR MORNING MEETING AND I HEARD THE MASTER RAISE HIS VOICE...

I'VE HAD ENOUGH OF THIS, HENRY. YOU WIN! IF YOU WOULD FURNISH ME ONLY THE COST OF AN EXPEDITION TO THE MOUNTAINS NEAR ALBANY, I SHALL FIND A TREASURE I ONCE HID THERE, AND SHALL BOTHER YOU NO MORE!

NOT A PENNY WILL I GIVE YOU... NOW OR EVER!

I MAKE MENTION OF THE FOREGOING INCIDENT BECAUSE IT WILL ILLUSTRATE HOW ABRUPT WAS MR. HENRY'S CHANGE OF OPINION FOLLOWING HIS READING OF A CERTAIN PAPER THAT HAD COME TO HAND SOME SHORT TIME AFTERWARD... AN ENGLISH PAMPHLET OF NEWS...

IS THERE NEWS COME FROM HOME, MR. HENRY?

OH... SOME LITTLE HERE AND THERE OF INTEREST...

AND THEN, LIKE A CLAP OF THUNDER, MR. HENRY'S VOICE ROARED OUT...

MACKELLAR! GET OUT!

Y-YES, MR. HENRY!

THE DOOR CLOSED AFTER ME AND I HEARD MRS. HENRY APPROACH. WE LOOKED WITH FRIGHT AT EACH OTHER, FOR WE THOUGHT FOR SURE IT MUST BE AN AWFUL BLOW THAT HAD COME...

WHAT CAN IT BE NOW? WHAT CAN IT BE?

SOME TIME LATER, I WAS SUMMONED TO MR. HENRY'S ROOM. FROM HIS FACE, THE LOOK OF FURY WAS GONE. IN ITS PLACE WAS A GRIM SMILE I DIDN'T LIKE...

DELIVER THIS LETTER, MACKELLAR, TO THE ONE TO WHOM IT IS ADDRESSED...

YES, MY LORD. I SHALL GO AT ONCE!

IT WAS TO GO TO A CAPTAIN HARRIS AND I WAS NOT AT ALL PLEASED WITH THE APPEARANCE OF THE MAN. HE HAD AN EVIL REPUTATION, MOREOVER, AS A PIRATE AND EVEN A MURDERER. AND TO MAKE THINGS WORSE, HE LATER CALLED AT THE HOME AND CONFERRED LONG AND CONFIDENTIALLY WITH MR. HENRY...

THEN IT'S AGREED. YOU'LL START AS SOON AS THINGS CAN BE ARRANGED.

AYE, THAT I WILL!

LATER, MR. HENRY LEFT THE ROOM. MUCH BEWILDERED, I BEGAN TO STRAIGHTEN UP THE DESK. A CRUMBLED NEWS PAMPHLET LAY THERE. I THOUGHT IT MIGHT HAVE HAD SOMETHING TO DO WITH THE RAGE OF MR. HENRY. I PERUSED THE PAPER AND FOUND THE FOLLOWING...

G POST NEW YORK.

Another notorious rebel, the M---r of B----e, is to have his title restored, since he rendered some services against Prince Charlie in favor of the Crown. His brother, L--d D---r is now to be set aside.

LONDON EVENING POST

NO ONE IN HIS RIGHT SENSES WOULD HAVE GIVEN THE ITEM A SECOND THOUGHT, SO PATENTLY FALSE WAS IT. IT WAS EITHER THE WORK OF SOME SCRIBBLER HACKING OUT COPY, OR --AS I SUSPECT-- THE WRITING OF THE MASTER HIMSELF, DONE TO WORRY MR. HENRY. IN ANY EVENT, A FEW DAYS LATER, THE MASTER WAS SETTING OUT FOR ALBANY WITH CAPTAIN HARRIS.

I WAS MUCH WORRIED AFTER THE DEPARTURE, MEDITATING ON THE STATE OF MR. HENRY'S LUNACY IN FINANCING SUCH A VENTURE. ON ARRIVING, I FOUND EVEN GREATER REASON FOR CONCERN...

YOU'RE PACKING, MR. HENRY. ARE YOU GOING AWAY?

INDEED. AND YOU, TOO, MACKELLAR. WE'RE GOING TO ALBANY...FOR A CHANGE OF SCENE!

I WILL PASS OVER THE FIRST OF OUR STAY IN ALBANY, AND WILL BEGIN WITH THE MISSION OF SIR WILLIAM JOHNSON TO TRAVEL INTO THE NEIGHBORHOOD OF LAKE CHAMPLAIN. I DO NOT KNOW HOW MR. HENRY ARRANGED TO GO ALONG, BUT WE WERE IN DUE TIME STARTING OUT FOR THE WILDERNESS...

WE HAD PROGRESSED FAR, WHEN THE ACTIONS OF MR. HENRY BEGAN TO WORRY ME. HE WOULD OFTEN APPROACH SIR WILLIAM...

I'VE A BROTHER HERE IN THESE WOODS. WILL YOU SEE IF THE SCOUTS HAVE FOUND HIM? IT IS VERY IMPORTANT TO ME!

THERE'S BEEN NO WORD, MR. DURIE!

FINALLY, SIR WILLIAM APPROACHED ME, AND I HAD TO ADMIT THAT I BELIEVED MR. HENRY'S MIND HAD BECOME AFFECTED...

IS IT SAFE, THEN, TO LET HIM GO AT LARGE?

THOSE WHO KNOW HIM BEST BELIEVE HE SHOULD BE SO HONORED, SIR WILLIAM.

WE HAD PROCEEDED INTO THIS SAVAGE COUNTRY FOR ABOUT A WEEK, WHEN ONE BITTERLY COLD MORNING, AS I WAS BUILDING UP THE FIRE BEFORE THE OTHERS HAD AWAKENED, I WAS STARTLED BY A MAN'S CRY.

HELP! HELP! HAVE YOU SEEN HIM? IS HE HERE?

IS WHO HERE? TO WHOM DO YOU REFER?

SECUNDRA DASS! WHERE IS HE? WHY DOES HE GO BACK AMONG THE DEAD? THERE'S SOME MYSTERY ABOUT HIM!

SPEAK MORE PLAINLY, MAN! WHO IS SECUNDRA DASS, ANYWAY?

THE MAN WAS JOHN MOUNTAIN OF THE MASTER'S SCOUTING PARTY. HE TOLD A STARTLING TALE THAT BEGAN WELL INSIDE THE WILDERNESS, TOO FAR FOR THE MASTER TO OBTAIN HELP IN HIS PLIGHT...

I TELL YOU, WE CAN'T KILL BALLANTRAE UNTIL WE KNOW THE LOCATION OF THE TREASURE!

WE CAN TORTURE THE TRUTH FROM HIM! SH-H! WHO IS BEHIND US?

§O THE MEN BURIED THE MASTER DEEP IN THE EARTH AND BETOOK THEMSELVES AWAY...

THE TREASURE IS NEAR HERE. I PROPOSE WE DO NOT LEAVE A STONE UNTURNED TO FIND IT!

§EARCH WAS UNSUCCESSFUL ON THE FIRST DAY. THE MEN RETIRED, EACH SUSPICIOUS OF THE OTHER, BUT TOO WEARY TO KEEP AWAKE. IN THE DEPTH OF THE NIGHT, A SHADOW STOLE UPON THEM...

THE NEXT MORNING, MOUNTAIN WAS THE FIRST TO ARISE. HIS HORRIBLE SCREAM AWAKENED THE CAMP...

SCALPED!

THE MEN LAID THE BLAME TO THEIR BEING UNSENTINELED. SO THEY SEARCHED FOR THE TREASURE ALL DAY, AND SLEEPING, LEFT A GUARD...

THE STARS SAY IT'S TIME TO CHANGE WATCH. I'LL GO WAKE HICKS SO HE CAN TAKE OVER.

ONLY HICKS' HEAD WAS SHOWING FROM OUT OF HIS BLANKET. THE SENTINEL PUT HIS HAND DOWN TO TOUCH HIM, AND PULLED IT BACK IN TERROR...

THE MEN, TERRIFIED, TOOK FLIGHT.

DEAD! NEXT IT WILL BE ME! I'M GOING CRAZY! CRAZY!

AT LAST BUT THREE WERE LEFT. AND THEN...

WE JOURNEYED SIXTEEN HOURS AND MADE CAMP FOR THE NIGHT. SOON WE WOULD BE UPON THE SCENE. I COULD NOT HELP BUT LOOK AT MY LORD AND BELIEVE THAT IN DEATH, THE MASTER WAS MORE AT PEACE...

SUDDENLY, MOUNTAIN SPRANG TO HIS FEET. AT ONCE, THE WHOLE CAMP WAS ALERT...

LISTEN! DO YOU HEAR THAT?

CLICK! DIG!

I HAVE IT! IT'S THAT INDIAN, SECUNDRA DASS! HE MUST KNOW WHERE THE TREASURE IS AND IS DIGGING IT UP!

OF COURSE! WE MIGHT HAVE EXPECTED THAT!

SHALL WE HAVE A MOON-LIGHT HUNT?

YES, LET US FIND SECUNDRA DASS!

WE MOVED CAUTIOUSLY TOWARD THE SOUND OF THE DIGGING AND INCH BY INCH WE APPROACHED, UNTIL AT LAST...

LOOK! LOOK!

THE INDIAN IS DIGGING UP THE BODY!

YOU SACRILEGIOUS HOUND!

WHAT'S THE MEANING OF THIS? WHAT DO YOU EXPECT TO GAIN BY SUCH AN ACT?

YOU WAIT SEE! YOU HELP! HIM BURY! HIM NOT DEAD!

WITH THAT, SECUNDRA DASS RECOGNIZED MR. HENRY AND ME. HIS VOICE ROSE TO A SHRIEK...

I TOLD YOU! DO YOU SEE NOW? HE IS NOT DEAD!

THERE MURDERERS! ALL MURDERERS! HIRE MURDERERS! I SAVE SAHIB; HE SEE ALL SWING IN A ROPE!

WHAT KIND OF RANT IS THIS?

COME, GIVE ME HELP! HIM BURY. HIM NOT DEAD!

UNDERSTAND, PLEASE! THE SAHIB ALONE WITH MURDERERS! TRY ESCAPE. NO WAY DO. I TRY THIS WAY. SWALLOW TONGUE! BURY ALIVE! GOOD WAY IN INDIA. HERE IN COLD, CAN'T TELL! HURRY NOW! YOU HELP! LIGHT FIRE!

WE ALL SET TO, EXCEPT MR. HENRY, WHO STOOD WATCHING AS ONE TRANSFIXED. SOON...

LOOK! WE'VE COME TO THE END OF THE DIGGING! HERE HE IS!

LOOK! HIS BEARD HAS GROWN! HIS FACE WAS SMOOTH WHEN WE BURIED HIM!

HURRY! HURRY! TAKE CLOSE TO FIRE!

ALL FELL TO AND WORKED FURIOUSLY, AS SECUNDRA DASS BREATHED IN THE MASTER'S MOUTH. I WAS TOO HORRIFIED TO TAKE PART. I STOOD BESIDE MR. HENRY, UNABLE TO MOVE...

SEE? SEE NOW? HE LIVE!

I WAS AMAZED AND HORRIFIED. THE LIDS FLICKERED FOR A MOMENT...

HELLO, MACKELLAR.

THEN I HEARD MR. HENRY CRY OUT. I TURNED TOWARD HIM, SAW HIM FALL DEAD!

THE MASTER DIED AT THE SAME MOMENT. DAY CAME AND STILL SECUNDRA DASS TRIED TO REVIVE HIM. ONE OF THE MEN WHO LEFT WITH ME WAS SKILLED IN STONE CUTTING. BEFORE SIR WILLIAM RETURNED TO PICK US UP, I HAD HIM CHISEL ON A BOULDER THIS INSCRIPTION-- WHICH MAY BE A FITTING END TO THIS NARRATIVE...

J.D.
HEIR TO A SCOTTISH TITLE. A MASTER IN THE ARTS AND GRACES ADMIRED IN EUROPE, ASIA, AMERICA, IN WAR AND PEACE, IN THE TENTS OF SAVAGE HUNTERS AND THE CITADELS OF KINGS, AFTER SO MUCH ACQUIRED, ACCOMPLISHED AND ENDURED, LIES HERE FORGOTTEN.

H.D.
HIS BROTHER. AFTER A LIFE OF UNMERITED DISTRESS BRAVELY SUPPORTED, DIED ALMOST IN THE SAME HOUR AND SLEEPS IN THE SAME GRAVE WITH HIS FRATERNAL ENEMY.

THE PIETY OF HIS WIFE AND ONE OLD SERVANT RAISED THIS STONE TO BOTH.

THE MASTER OF BALLANTRAE

ROBERT LOUIS STEVENSON

A black winter's night. A lonely place. The clash of swords in anger: a duel between brothers. One falls, killed, it seems, by the other, who walks away. In a moment of high drama, the long enmity between them seems to have

reached its climax and conclusion: a miserable end for the loser, but victory and vindication for the other, so long the patient victim of fraternal persecution. We'd be satisfied with such a conclusion, perhaps, which leaves the wicked James suitably punished for his crimes and the virtuous, long-suffering Henry with the chance of a happy future. We've all seen the like many times. It's a commonplace of books and movies and bad television.

But that's not the story Robert Louis Stevenson is telling. No such easy triumph will resolve the battle between good and evil embodied by the two brothers Durie. The duel ends nothing. The "dead" man will return to torment his family again. And

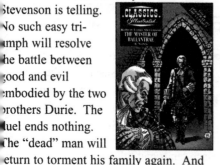

the virtue of his "killer" will prove to be a frailer thing than we had comfortably been assuming. In *The Master of Ballantrae* Stevenson seems at first to be giving us another rip-roaring adventure of similar spirit to *Kidnapped* or *Treasure Island,* but this is a much darker tale than those, with a much grimmer core, akin to the dire pessimism of *Dr. Jekyll and Mr. Hyde.* There is no victory for the virtuous here, but destruction. The evil, charming Master of Ballantrae may lose his life in the end, but not before he has succeeded in the struggle for his brother's soul.

What makes a good man good? What can make a good man bad? We throw around such labels with ease, but can the motives of the human heart really be defined as "good" or "bad" with any certainty? *The Master of Ballantrae* asks us these questions, and invites us to study them. It does not give us easy answers.

THE AUTHOR

Robert Louis Stevenson

Robert Louis Stevenson was born in Edinburgh, Scotland, in 1850, the son of a prosperous engineer in a family of light-housebuilders. A sickly child, his adoring parents regularly took him abroad on holidays for his health. His father had assumed he would pursue the family profession, but that didn't suit his health or interests and he enrolled as a law student at the University of Edinburgh. It turned out that didn't suit him either. He skipped classes, lived idly, and quarreled with his father. In the 1870's he traveled repeatedly in France for his health and began to write professionally — first essays, then fiction. It was on one of his trips to France that he met Mrs. Fanny Osbourne, a married American woman with two children, whom he stayed with for several summers. After she returned to California to begin divorce proceedings, Stevenson followed, and in 1880 they married.

Over the following years he was increasingly successful as a writer. *Treasure Island* was serialized in a children's magazine in 1881-82, and more novels followed, including *The Strange Case of Dr. Jekyll and Mr. Hyde* (1886), *Kidnapped* (1886) and its sequel *David Balfour* (1893), *The Black Arrow* (1888), and *The Master of Ballantrae* (1889), along with many stories, poetry, essays, plays, and travel books. But illness dogged him, particularly tuberculosis. At times he was completely bedridden. His health was always better at sea; he and Fanny traveled widely, and in 1888 they journeyed for the first time to the South Seas, visiting Tahiti, Hawaii, and the Marquesas. He loved the climate, the places, the people of the Pacific. On the way home to Europe, serious illness struck him again in Sydney and the doctors ordered him to remain in the tropics; so he and Fanny settled in Samoa, to be joined by other members of his family and a steady stream of visiting friends and admirers. He continued to write and publish. His last novel, *Weir of Hermiston,* was unfinished when he died of a stroke in 1894.

CHARACTER AND PLOT
A Family at War

At its heart, *The Master of Ballantrae* is a study of characters and their relationships. The cast is small — barely half a dozen individuals have more than a casual role — and of these, several, including the elder Lord Durrisdeer and the Master's Indian companion Secundra Dass, are shadowy figures whose personality and motives are never fully revealed or examined. The central participants in the tale, however, are explored in depth, and with great subtlety.

The family Durie was, we are told, of old Scottish nobility, but by the mid-1700's when the story takes place they have lost most of their wealth, and with it their political importance.

Lord Durrisdeer, the head of the family, is a prematurely aged man when we first meet him, and one who has done a poor job both in sustaining the family's property and pretensions, and in raising his two sons. The elder and favorite is **James Durie, Master of Ballantrae**. Brought up as the heir to lands and title, he is destined by is father to marry his orphaned cousin Alison so that her wealth can restore the family's battered fortune. Even before the opening of the story he is a wild young man with a reputation for drinking, gambling, brawling, and womanizing. Among the common people of the district his display of aristocratic carelessness made him a figure of admiration. He is charming and raffish, equally at home among gentlemen and smugglers, quick to endear himself to the powerful, quick to turn even the most unpromising situation to his advantage, and leaves his companions to face the consequences.

The Master's dominant trait is his selfishness. As a youth he let nothing stand between him and his pleasures; as a grown man that continues to be true. He has no sense of responsibility toward others, but acts only to gratify his own whims and desires, regardless of the cost to anyone else. In this spirit he overthrows his father's cautious plan in the crisis of 1745: the younger son shall join the rebellion while the elder stays behind at home. That doesn't suit the Master's adventurous temper. He has to play the hero, lead the local men off to war, and display his reckless courage to impress the public (and his cousin Alison) despite the risks his involvement in a treasonous escapade create for the family. Once among the rebels he insinuates himself in the favor of Bonnie Prince Charlie, encouraging the reckless prince's most grandiose dreams to the neglect of sound strategy, and so

contributes directly to the disastrous defeat at Culloden — at which time he has no other thought but to save his own skin. Rescued, then captured by pirates, he immediately joins them, standing by while his shipmates of a few minutes before are forced to walk the plank. The Master not only participates in their crimes but makes himself their leader — until the moment arrives that he can betray them in turn, and abscond with most of their stolen money in safety.

The Master is an opportunist. Treachery and deceit are as natural for him as breathing. His thoughts rarely extend beyond his self-interest. It never occurs to him, for instance, to inform his family he hadn't died at Culloden, until he needs their money. In his relentless demand for funds he never cares how he might be draining the family's resources, but simply sucks up everything his brother can send and insists on more, till he has consumed as much as he's allowed of the property (as well as Alison's inheritance). Thwarted, he becomes vengeful. When he returns home he plays on his father's and Alison's affections by showing them his most charming face, but torments his brother unmercifully in private, and finally provokes him to a duel. And in that encounter he shows how single-minded he is about winning, how completely devoid of honor, by trying to cheat.

His trick fails, and he loses the fight — is killed, it is thought at first. He pursues his fortune elsewhere till new reverses in India turn him back to Scotland once again, and on to New York in pursuit of his brother. By now a man in his forties, he has not changed at all over the years. Still selfish, immature, vengeful, and empty of heart, he can present himself with so much charm and plausible smoothness that even his brother's loyal henchman Mackellar, who knows every detail of his past misbehavior, is seduced for a time and wavers in his conviction.

At last he reaches the limits of his ability to glide out of harm's way. In New York it is his brother Henry who has the upper hand. His intentions are still bad, but circumstances turn against him: from being the persecutor, he is now the victim of persecution and fraternal treachery. And still he will not yield to anyone else's will, will not bend to anyone else's demands, not content himself with any future but the one he makes for himself. In the minds of others he has assumed almost the status of a force of nature, uncontrollable and destructive in its freedom. He has cheated death so often that it hardly seems possible in the end that he can't weasel out of it one more time. Like the villain in a slasher movie, you have to actually see him dead and buried and still in the ground to know it's over.

Even then, Secundra Dass (for one) expects him to rise again.

The Master's evil takes many forms. Besides his readiness to lie and cheat and betray anyone he has the chance to, he shows a casual disregard for human life. When he encounters Burke fleeing the defeat at Culloden he leaves it to the toss of a coin to decide whether they are to fight or join forces. Among the pirates he is as violent as any, and maintains his dominance by brutality as well as cleverness. He conspires with Teach to steal the pirates' treasure, and betrays him. He gets two of the pirates to help his escape across the marsh, and neither one lives to reach solid land. His conduct toward women is detestable. He delights in toying with Alison's affections, using her love as a weapon against his brother. He does not seem to have strong feelings for anyone at all, only the art of pretending them at will. He shows that behind the pleasant surface of the world lies only corruption and emptiness.

Ballantrae's younger brother **Henry Durie** presents a far less seductive appearance. Henry doesn't have any of the Master's showy qualities. He is quiet, shy, studious, dutiful, a dull stick by contrast with his flashy, extroverted brother. He is neglected and disparaged by both his father and Alison. When the Master rides out heroically to join Bonnie Prince Charlie, he's acclaimed by the neighborhood, while Henry, obliged to seek favor from the English authorities to protect the family's future, is scorned by his own tenants. His virtues are unspectacular ones — honesty, diligence, responsibility, devotion to his family, attention to business. He does everything a loyal son, husband, and landlord could be expected to, and no one except his servant Mackellar recognizes or appreciates it. While his brother roams the world, Henry stays at home. He sends the Master large sums of money on demand; when the continual hemorrhage of funds undermines the health of the family's resources, he tries to cover it and hide the cause; when he tries to reduce spending and increase the income from the estates, they think he's being stingy and grasping. Honor and pride keep him silent about the truth. He seems as convinced as the rest of his own inherent unworthiness. Since he has skulked at home like a coward and let his brother ride in his place to war and exile, has stolen his brother's promised bride and usurped his inheritance, is it not a just punishment that his brother should secretly harass and torment him, and that no one else should know of it?

Henry's long silent endurance of the Master's persecution ends on the night of the duel: all the secrets are finally revealed to the rest. But that night also marks another change — for Henry has at last responded to the Master's jibes with violence of his own and has tried to kill his brother (successfully, he thinks at first). This signals an inner degradation of his character which will gradually become more and more apparent. For years Henry feared and hated the Master. Now he is obsessed with him. Even as his wife, waking from her blind infatuation, turns a more loving eye to her husband, he becomes neglectful, not even aware of the affection he formerly craved. Embittered, he grows petty and vengeful, convinced that the Master embodies super-human Evil and that only extreme measures can thwart his malice. His virtues have been corrupted, his mind grown unbalanced, his plodding temperament grown whimsical and odd.

Mackellar claims this is the effect of the fever which afflicted him after the duel, but this is not a complete or convincing explanation. Henry's personality has never been a strong one, and now it is crumbling from within.

The arrival of the Master after the collapse of his Indian ventures galvanizes Henry into new activity. He sees the Master as a monster of villainy, so the prospect of his influence on the son Henry dotes on terrifies him beyond reason. He makes and executes his plans with masterful speed. But beyond removing his family and wealth physically beyond the Master's reach, what does he hope to accomplish by fleeing to New York? It's unclear, but certainly he can't have been surprised that his brother, who can't stand being frustrated at the last minute, *has* to follow. The new environment gives Henry an advantage; arriving first, he doesn't hesitate to shape public opinion in his favor against a sibling no one knows. The events which follow, however, show just how far he has fallen from his earlier honorable character. It's he, now, who plays the bully and tormentor. When the penniless Master sets himself up on public display, Henry feels none of the shame the charade was supposed to produce in him, but on the contrary takes great pleasure in seeing his brother humiliate himself. And in the end it's Henry, not the Master, who plots fratricide with a gang of villains, and hires them to lure his brother into the wilderness to be murdered.

Though the plan goes awry, it's not because Henry has had second thoughts. He has no thought now at all except his brother's death. Consumed with hatred and fear he has become a monster even more dangerous than the object of his obsession. All his virtue and goodness is corroded and transformed into its opposite. At the end, he's just the shell of himself. He has become as bad as his brother, or worse — vile and degraded without even the benefit of the Master's charm and energy.

Of the other characters in the novel, most are only present for a scene or two, and are more vivid than deep. **Captain Teach**, for instance, is a bully and a drunkard, who rules his pirate crew by bluff and violence. He is happy to conspire with the Master to cheat them and steal the treasure, but naïve enough to expect the Master won't betray him, in turn, the minute it suits him. **Alison Durie** is in view throughout the novel, but mostly in the background, and we only see her from the outside, in the context of her relationship with Henry and the Master. As a romantic young girl she fell in love with the Master and disdains the dull younger brother she married for the sake of the family. Throughout the first years of the marriage she ignores her husband's craving for her attention. The

shock of the duel and its aftermath bring them into closer sympathy for a while, but after the birth of her son she finds *herself* the neglected partner, helpless to do anything but observe Henry's mental and moral decay. While she is strong-willed and passionate, she has little scope for action, let alone initiative, as the struggle between the brothers unfolds, and her role as a passive bystander, or worse, as a prize in contention between them, is not one that makes her particularly lovable or sympathetic in the reader's eyes.

On the other hand **Colonel Burke**, the professional soldier whose Memoirs give us most of our information about the Master during his absences, *is* a likable figure largely because he does take action and stands up for himself. Burke is a romantic Irishman who seems in truth very much the hearty and simple person he appears to be. He is accustomed to judging situations and people by appearances; he doesn't delve deep into hidden motives, and treachery in his companions always surprises him. He would rather play the fool than the villain. Unlike many of those around him he has a clear sense of right and wrong, even though his behavior doesn't always live up to his own standards and he is susceptible to the influence of a dominant personality like the Master's. But there are transgressions he won't accept, even from the Master. He plays an equivocal role after the Master's first return to Europe, carrying his initial demands to Scotland for him, but also alerting the family to the Master's true circumstances. After the Master betrays him in India,

The Forty-Five

The roots of the Scottish rising of 1745 stretch back to 1603, when the Scottish king James VI inherited the English throne and moved south to reign as James I. The Scots retained a sentimental attachment to the Stuart dynasty, but the English didn't. In 1688, fearful for the survival of their Protestant religion when the Catholic James II became the father of a Catholic heir, the English deposed the king, who fled with his family to France. The crowns of England and Scotland passed to his Protestant daughters, and in 1714 to a German Protestant cousin, George I. The son of James II was excluded from the royal succession because he refused to renounce his Catholic faith. He continued to claim the throne, however, and became known as the **Old Pretender**. His son Charles Edward Stuart was called the **Young Pretender**, or more colorfully, **Bonnie Prince Charlie**. Their supporters were **Jacobites** ("Jacob" being a Latinate form of "James"). Neither Charles Edward nor his younger brother ever married, and the direct Stuart line died with them.

By the Act of Union in 1707 Scotland surrendered its political independence, including the right to determine its own kings, in exchange for full participation in the growing British Empire. The Scots were not consulted on the succession of George I, and many resented it, as well as other high-handed policies and taxes imposed on them from London. In 1715 a rebellion in the name of the Old Pretender collapsed quickly and the prince returned to exile, while a handful of rebels were executed and the rest went home quietly.

The Jacobite cause languished until, in the 1740's, the French government (then at war with Britain) provided funds and encouragement to revive it. In 1745 Bonnie Prince Charlie, a handsome, brave, and romantic young man without much political or military talent, landed in Scotland and quickly raised the clans of the Highlands to support him. They marched first into Edinburgh, then south into England, defeating the first English force sent against them; but early delays gave the English time to mobilize larger armies against the invaders. The Scots had gotten within a hundred miles of London when the prince's advisors persuaded him to retreat before he was surrounded and

IT WAS A BITTER DISAPPOINTMENT FOR THE PRINCE, FOR THE JACOBITES WERE SCARCELY READY...

I'D LIKE TO SEE THE BONNIE PRINCE ENTHRONED, BUT I SCARCE CAN RISK MY HEAD ON A CHANCE OF VICTORY!

NOR I. THE PRINCE HAS BUT FOUR THOUSAND MEN. 'TIS NOT ENOUGH.

cut off. The Jacobite army withdrew into Scotland and back to the Highlands, dwindling all the time. In April 1746 they were defeated by the Duke of Cumberland at Culloden Moor.

Bonnie Prince Charlie escaped and after many adventures reached safety in France, but his followers suffered bloody reprisals. Throughout the Highlands, farms and villages were burnt, hundreds were imprisoned and executed for treason or transported to the American colonies, property was confiscated and handed out to strangers, and traditional institutions were suppressed. English policy aimed to break the power of the clans and their leaders, and incidentally to assimilate the Highlanders into "civilized" society by attempting to restrict the use of the Gaelic language and outlaw other elements of their distinctive culture like the wearing of tartans.

The Forty-Five failed in large part because the majority of Scots, even those dissatisfied with the English regime, did not actively support it. But in failure the '45 entered Scottish popular memory as a glorious romantic cause; support for the Stuarts came to represent the yearning for a lost golden age of honor, loyalty, and community, all of which by 1800 seemed threatened by the transforming power of industrialization, and soon, by liberal democracy. It remains a touchstone of Scottish national identity and myth.

Burke condemns him roundly; such a violation of friendship is about the only thing he finds truly unforgivable.

Mackellar, the Durrisdeer secretary and man-of-business, is a more interesting character, not least because it's through his eyes that we see most of the story, and through his narrative filter that we encounter the rest. He's a fussy, pedantic, painstaking man who openly declares his sympathy for his employer Henry Durie against anyone else. He shares the secret of the Master's long harassment of his brother, and of Henry's financial maneuvers to meet those demands and hide the cost to the estate. He's the middleman in all the transactions between the brothers. When the Master returns home Mackellar is the only witness to the private unpleasantness between them, and to the duel by candlelight which ends in the Master's supposed death. Mackellar himself comes in for his share of the Master's teasing and taunting as well, mostly in ways which emphasize his inferior status as a servant and his physical cowardice, a characteristic which would have been deeply shaming to a gentleman. So his intense partisanship on Henry's behalf is not entirely selfless. When the Master's final reappearance in Scotland prompts Henry's midnight flight with his family and assets to New York, Mackellar takes rather cruel

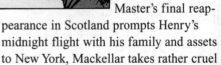

FOR WEEKS, MR. HENRY HOVERED BETWEEN LIFE AND DEATH. THEN, ONE DAY, HIS EYES OPENED WITH SOME LIGHT OF INTELLIGENCE. HE LOOKED AT MRS. HENRY WITHOUT RECOGNITION, HOWEVER, AND THEN TURNED TO ME...

MACKELLAR! MY OLD FRIEND!

OH, MR. HENRY! YOU RECOGNIZED ME!

pleasure in revealing the trick to the Master and dictating the humiliating terms for his future maintenance.

But then, on the stormy voyage they share across the Atlantic, their relationship takes an unexpected turn. Forced to deal with the Master in close quarters for weeks on end, Mackellar discovers that the demonic figure of earlier encounters is just a man after all, and one who is charming, witty, intelligent, even admirable in some ways. The Master, in need of allies at this point in his career, is clearly exerting himself to seduce Mackellar's loyalty, even his affection, away from Henry. By the time they reach New York he has largely succeeded. Mackellar, for his part, knows what's going on. He never abandons Henry entirely, nor does he forget that the Master's past record of actions proves a selfish, cunning, and vicious nature lies behind the ingratiating manners and superficial attractiveness. But he can no longer pretend that all the blame for the continuing trouble lies entirely on the Master's side, nor ignore the mounting signs that Henry's obsession with his brother has taken a virulent and self-destructive turn. It is a sign of Mackellar's weakness that, knowing all this, he takes no steps to intervene between them, but allows the affair to move toward what he knows what must be a fatal conclusion.

All his adult life Mackellar has been a servant, loyal and hardworking, doing as he was bidden. He has been an observer of the brothers' quarrel, but only an incidental participant. Now, when true service would have meant refusing orders and interfering to frustrate his master's intentions, he shrinks back and lets events take their course. His cowardice rears its head again: he doesn't have the nerve to do more than observe and comment. The outcome is desolation.

SETTINGS
A Wide and Restless World

In its preoccupation with the inner demons of the human spirit, *The Master of Ballantrae* is a companion-piece to *Dr. Jekyll and Mr. Hyde* among Stevenson's works. The activity of the plot, however, would seem to place it closer on the shelf to his popular adventure-stories, like *Treasure Island* and *Kidnapped*. It shares many familiar elements with those favorites, and with other novels its readers would have known. The scene of the action is constantly shifting and busy, and the narrators change also, as Mackellar adds the testimony of men like Burke and Mountain to his own account. The result is an extremely colorful, restless succession of episodes, which give the story almost a kaleidoscopic quality. The intense activity, though, is partly illusory. The complexity of the text is compounded by the fractured, unreliable narrative voice.

The opening scenes site the novel in Scotland during the Jacobite rebellion of 1745. (NOTE: see The Forty-Five) This was familiar ground for readers of historical fiction, ever since Sir Walter Scott invented the genre with his Jacobite adventure *Waverley* in 1814. Stevenson had already dealt with it himself in *Kidnapped*; in fact, his character Alan Breck Stewart from that novel makes a cameo appearance here. The 1745 rebellion, and the Jacobite cause in general, were highly romanticized in nineteenth-century fiction as doomed, glorious adventures. Stevenson's approach here contradicts that view. The cautious decision of Lord Durrisdeer to send one son to the rebellion and the other to butter up the established authorities shows the ambivalence and compromising response of many landed families, who had to protect their long-term interests regardless of their emotional response to the situation. That the Master rejects his father's plan and impulsively demands as a matter of pride to lead the local men to war demonstrates at the very start of the tale his rash and selfish character; while the weakness and partiality of other members of the family are clear in their reactions. In the eyes of Lord Durrisdeer and Alison, the headstrong, dashing James can do no wrong, while plodding, dutiful Henry can never be good enough to please them. The unfairness is only compounded by the general scorn heaped on Henry by the tenants for doing his family duty and collaborating with the victorious English, and for remaining alive when his heroic brother has (as everyone thought) died in the glorious disaster of Culloden.

The scene, in Burke's narrative, shifts from the battlefield to the high seas. Pirate stories were another staple of adventure fiction. (NOTE: see Pirates) *Treasure Island,* one of the definitive tales of the genre, had been Stevenson's first great success as a novelist, and pirates continued to be popular with readers (as in Rafael Sabatini's *Captain Blood*, or James Barrie's *Peter Pan*). When Stevenson revisits this setting in *The Master of Ballantrae*, though, he gives us a much grimmer portrayal than the usual romanticized fare. Teach's pirates are not in the least bit noble or admirable or even really interesting; they're a brutal, drunken rabble who can barely handle their own ship, much less seize a prize or avoid capture. They fall easily under the sway of the Master, who ingratiates himself with the crew in much the same way he had with Bonnie Prince Charlie and uses them to his own profit. His betrayal of the pirates, and of those who thought they were his partners in treachery, shows his greed and opportunism in their rawest form, without any gloss of civility or necessity.

The Master's involvement in the '45 has marked him in law as a traitor and a fugitive, so he can't return home and reclaim his inheritance; but once he has returned to France he sends Burke to Scotland with news of his survival and

Pirates

As long as there have been ships, there have been pirates. The Romans fought them in the Mediterranean. The first foreign war of the infant U.S. was against the Barbary Pirates of Algiers. They are a major threat to shipping today in the South China Sea. The classic pirates of swashbuckling fiction, however, were those of the Caribbean who flourished in the decades around 1700.

Many of these pirates started out as "privateers," licensed by a government (usually the French or English) to attack ships belonging to the enemy in time of war. Some stayed within the letter of their commission; others became free agents, going after any target that presented itself. After the wars between France and England concluded in 1713, British authorities intensified their campaign to clear the sea of pirates, and by 1730 were largely successful. Edward Teach, aka Blackbeard, terrorized the Carolina coast for several years before he was killed in 1718. The celebrated Captain Kidd, most of whose buried treasure is supposedly still waiting discovery near Long Island Sound, was initially part of this anti-piracy campaign until he switched sides; once captured, he was taken to London and hanged after a well-publicized trial.

A lot of our popular image of pirates comes from romantic fiction like *Treasure Island, Captain Blood,* and *Peter Pan,* and from colorful movies inspired by them. When we hear "pirate" we typically imagine figures like Long John Silver or Captain Hook, complete with cutlasses and parrots, ordering their captives to walk the plank. Recent research, including archaeological work on the wrecks of pirate ships, has uncovered much of the truth behind the legends. Pirates really did fly the "Jolly Roger" with the skull-and-crossbones, but they used many other symbols too, like bleeding hearts, swords, and hourglasses. They didn't make people "walk the plank" either — guns and swords were quicker and more efficient for killing prisoners, while some pirates treated their captives well, to encourage future enemies to surrender rather than fight to the death. Pirates prized money and jewels, but their typical plunder consisted mostly of silk or cotton cloth, tobacco, and ship's supplies. Pirate crews were commonly democratic societies which elected their own captains and quartermasters. The loot would be divided almost equally, too, which meant that precious items like jewelry were often broken up into pieces. On most pirate ships were men of many nations, who might have previously served on several different ships. At least a quarter of them were former slaves. A few were women. Regardless of origin or gender, they commonly came to violent ends, even when they evaded capture and execution.

the first of his demands for funds, which Henry unhappily complies with. For years the Master drains the wealth of the estate like a vampire sucking his victim's blood. Only after Henry finally refuses to continue paying him, and his own need for money is acute, does he return in person to his family. This visit is a sustained exercise in duplicity and hypocrisy, which culminates in the midnight duel.

That battle by candlelight between brothers stands as a moment of high drama in the grand tradition, violent and tragic in its consequences. The Master's startling disappearance is as shocking to us as to the participants. Its explanation, that he was rescued from the scene by the same smugglers who had brought him home in the first place, reminds us of his chameleon-like ability to be at ease in any society; his ease with inferiors always presents a marked contrast to his brother's stiffness and withdrawal, which is so often seen as arrogance. The Master automatically

tries to charm anyone who can be useful to him. Conversely, he doesn't hesitate to dump anyone who isn't. We see this when Burke meets him again in India; Burke is in danger and needs his help, but the Master rejects his former friend completely, even denying that they speak the same language! Self-interest has leached all natural feeling out of the Master's heart, leaving only the knowledge how to use it against others when the opportunity comes.

We never find out much about the Master's activities in India, except that he established himself in the entourage of French empire-builders, and consequently lost everything when they were driven out by the British. In nineteenth-century British fiction India often figures as a place where fortunes were easily won and lost. More generally it represented the mysterious, the exotic, and the uncanny; the ordinary rules of European civilization didn't quite apply there, and both the people and their culture were incomprehensible to most Europeans. In fiction, Indians in Europe often figured as the agents of mysterious fate, like the guardians of the stolen diamond in Wilkie Collins's *The Moonstone*, or the benevolent servant Ram Dass who helps restore the orphaned Sara Crewe to happiness in Frances Hodgson Burnett's *A Little Princess*. Secundra Dass, the Master's devoted companion in the later sections of the story, is another such mysterious figure; without doing anything overtly vilainous himself except eavesdropping, he s sinister by implication and association. t's appropriate that we never learn exactly vhat bond exists between the Master and Secundra, or the circumstances that brought them togeth-er; if the Master were truly an agent of the devil, as Henry seems to believe, Secundra might be his familiar, an enabler of evil. Certainly his love for the Master and his confidence in the Master's abilities are powerful; only death can part them.

For its final episodes the story travels again, to New York and to the hostile wilderness beyond. Once again, these are settings which would have been familiar to Stevenson's readers from other popular historical novels, particularly those of James Fenimore Cooper (*The Deerslayer, The Pathfinder, The Last of the Mohicans,* etc.) which were similarly set in the mid-1700's. The setting was more than a nar-rative convenience for Stevenson, howev-er, nor color for its own sake. It was dur-ing a winter visit to a health resort on Lake Saranac in the Adirondacks that he first conceived the images and characters that turned into this novel. And just as India, in Victorian fictional codes, hinted at mysterious knowledge and diabolical powers — all the evils of decadent ancient civilization — so the American wilderness represented the casting-off of civilization, stripping characters and setting to elemen-tal basics. Virtue and villainy stand, theo-retically, in sharper relief *without* the superficial gloss of manners and polite hypocrisy — reduced to their essentials by more fundamental struggles for survival and dominance.

In the city of New York, Henry uses the trappings of civiliza-tion, his economic power and political connections, to thwart his brother's schemes. The Master in turn hopes that by violating social conventions he can shame Henry into different behavior. For the brutal conclu-sion, however, both men have to abandon the settled world and confront nature and its agents directly. And which of them, in this final juncture, is the more savage, less an exemplar of civilized virtue or natural nobility of the spirit? It is the last tragic irony of the tale that what might once have been an obvious answer is no longer so. Neither brother can ever return from the wilderness of the soul which has claimed them both.

THEME AND VOICE
Jekyll and Hyde Revisited

Beneath all the frenetic action which carries the events of the plot from one continent to another, the story of *The Master of Ballantrae* follows a straight-forward progression, or rather *descent*, in its tone. As episode follows episode, the violence which marks them all becomes inexorably more brutal, the struggle between the brothers more personal and intimate. The Master attacks Henry by claiming "his" share of the family wealth; Henry eventually retaliates by withholding it. They compete for the affections of neighbors, and more fiercely for those of the family. The Master has always been their father's favorite; Henry throws that bitterly in his face. (See previous page). More wounding, the Master has early on assured himself of Alison's love; Henry knows it, and even after they have been married for years the warmth she still cherishes for his brother adds fuel and flame to their rivalry. In contrast, he dotes on his son to the point others worry he'll repeat his father's mistake and spoil the child. It's the threat the Master's seduction poses to his son that tips him into desperation. In New York, finally, the brothers have to grapple with each other directly, one man trying to break the will and spirit of the other, with no one and nothing standing between them. As the layers of social convention and family are stripped away, good and evil become less and less distinguishable.

This gradual darkening of mood is echoed by the gradual corruption of personal relations that accompanies Henry's moral disintegration. He starts out as a loving son and devoted husband, though neither father nor wife return his feelings as they ought. He spares no effort to protect them from all outside threats, and from the selfish, irresponsible Master. Bit by bit, however, his obsession with the wrongs he has suffered transforms him. He becomes deceitful, secretive, impatient, unable to tolerate frustration: "alternately the ostrich and the bull" when thwarted, as Mackellar says. After the birth of his son and heir he has no thought for anyone else, neglecting wife, friends, and business in his "slavery to the child." He has come to imagine his brother an agent of the devil, if not a devil himself, endowed with magical vitality and supernatural powers of evil. In a state of near panic he flees to New York, dragging wife and children at his heels.

He no longer simply wants to avoid contact with his brother, he wants to *hurt* him. In New York he relishes the Master's humiliation. Shamelessly, he goes daily to watch the Master display himself as a tailor, intent upon adding to his torment by gloating. Reproached by Mackellar for his vindictive behavior, he is unrepentant. "I grow fat upon it," he says. Mackellar is shocked by both the words and Henry's willing indulgence in "hateful pleasures," obvious signs of his moral collapse. They have the intended effect on the Master, whose flight into the wilderness to reclaim his long-buried treasure is a frank admission of defeat. But that is not enough for Henry. He has fallen so low that he hires a gang of thugs to murder

I VIEWED MR. HENRY FROM AFAR AND SAW, TO MY HORROR, THAT HE HAD COME TO STARE WITH A CERTAIN GRINNING RELISH AT THE MASTER IN HIS STATE OF POVERTY. I GASPED, FOR I REALIZED IT WAS HATE NOT LOVE THAT BROUGHT HIM OUT EACH DAY WITH A REGULARITY THAT HAD BECOME RITUAL ...

is brother; in in the end, nothing will satisfy him but to see his brother's dead body with his own eyes. Having abandoned and defied every ordinary tie of affection to family and friends, he insists on this last proof of his own fall, and he dies at the sight of it.

The text of *The Master of Ballantrae* is less straightforward than its subject. It is a tricky document, because Stevenson makes deliberate use of a series of unreliable narrators to tell the story, and repeatedly throws us off balance when we've gotten too comfortable. Mackellar, the most consistent voice through the novel, is overtly partisan, seeking to show Henry in the most flattering light and the Master in the worst. At first we take him at his word, but it becomes clear he is not always sure of the facts. He reports the most complex episodes in ambiguous terms, especially as the story develops and his own loyalties are challenged. What, for instance, *really* happened during the duel? At times he highlights his own lack of direct information and conflicted feelings to distance himself and us from the events he records. At others he gives us the illusion of impartial observation; but his selective account is never impartial. His cowardice and timidity color all his responses to the Master, who is physically bold and masterful in temper; besides the fear and antagonism he evokes, in Mackellar's dealings with him there's always a measure of awe, which contributes to his larger-than-life persona. And when Mackellar is thrust into the Master's company for the first time on the stormy voyage to New York, his hostility softens under the onslaught of the Master's insistent charm: a weakness which embarrasses him and colors all the rest of the tale with ambivalence.

How are we to interpret the events of the story, and judge the characters, when even our guide has only a confused idea of the truth?

We hear from other voices as well, but in these cases too Mackellar's presence as editor shapes the text. He gives us extracts of Burke's memoirs, but is never far away himself, with fussy footnotes commenting on Burke's narrative and correcting some small points. This presumably implies the accuracy of the rest, which includes the most highly-colored and exotic scenes of the book: the tale of the pirates, the Master's first difficult journey through the Adirondacks, and his later encounter with Burke in India. Mackellar indeed comments explicitly that certain passages he omits were unbelievable, though he is clearly applying a different standard than we would. He remarks at length, for instance, on an account Burke gives of a quarrel between himself and the Master in the wilderness, which is not given in the text; Mackellar says that it "is really more than I can reproduce; for I knew the Master myself, and a man more insusceptible of fear is not conceivable. I regret this oversight of [Burke's], and all the more because the tenor of his narrative (set aside a few flourishes) strikes me as highly ingenuous."

Mackellar, in other words, vouches for the truth of *most* of the story. But if Burke's testimony is not reliable in all its parts, if he misrepresents or misremembers certain elements, why should we simply accept Mackellar's judgment about the rest?

And when we come to the "narrative" of the frontiersman Mountain telling of the Master's last journey into the wilderness with Secundra Dass and Henry's hired assassins, what Mackellar gives us is not even the man's own words, but a frankly speculative account compiled from a variety of sources. How far can we trust it on any of the details, when even something as crucial as the circumstances of the Master's death — indeed, the very fact of his death itself — is ambiguous and uncertain, and all the sources have been further strained through the filter of Mackellar's prejudices? The episode becomes virtually a fiction within the fiction. The reader can disregard any element of this most fantastic segment of the story which seems to push the boundaries of belief too far. The occasional intervention of yet another, external editor distances us even further from the events, and adds another layer of ambiguity. We are left, in the end, with a series of possibilities, but no firm grip on the "truth," if indeed there is any such thing here.

The straightforward surface of this novel folds back, then, to reveal an extremely complex narrative structure. The effect, in a story dealing explicitly with the nature of human good and human evil, is to keep the reader off-balance by a constant, subtle shifting of the moral ground. The ambivalence of Mackellar's attitudes over the course of the story keeps yanking us back to question what's really going on, and why. In *Dr. Jekyll and Mr. Hyde,* Stevenson used the mechanism of a chemical potion to split the good and evil impulses of a normal man into separate entities, both pure and incomplete. The horror of Mr. Hyde is not so much his brief and violent existence, but the idea of his concealed presence within each one of us. In *The Master of Ballantrae,* Stevenson approaches the same idea from a different perspective. The gradual, inexorable corruption of the honorable Henry Durie is even more painful than what befell Dr. Jekyll because it comes solely from within.

Stevenson himself conceived the story of *The Master of Ballantrae* in stark terms. He saw the Master in his wickedness as an incubus, a demon, sucking out the virtue of his younger brother; readers were supposed to approve of the murder at the conclusion as a suitable punishment for his evil. The story Stevenson actually wrote is more interesting precisely because the lines between good and evil have been blurred. The Master himself is no one-dimensional bogey man, but a vibrant being, energetic and unrepentant from beginning to end. The urges that drive him from one act of villainy to another spring not from blind, bland malevolence, but from his hunger for excitement and adventure, and his determination never to be thwarted or let any setback get the better of him for long. Time and time again he runs headlong into some catastrophe which costs him everything, and every time but the last he manages by ingenuity and force of will to turn fate around and create new opportunities for himself. To be sure, his methods are frequently horrifying, and reveal a selfish and morally bankrupt nature. His incessant demands on the family estate are motivated as much by a desire for revenge as by simple greed or necessity. He has no conscience, only a keen sense of what is convenient. He can justify even the most despicable conduct on the grounds of necessity or right.

And that is one of the things that makes him such an unforgettable character. Although he is obviously a villain of monstrous depravity, he sees himself as the hero, wronged by the world without having done anything to deserve it, and therefore released from the rules that limit the behavior of others. He is above all an *active* character. His role in the tale is shaped by his own choices, his unbroken will.

The "good" brother Henry, in contrast, starts out passive. He reacts to his brother, to his father and Allison, to information brought by Burke, smugglers, newspapers, others; but he almost never takes the initiative himself. His virtue is also passive. He is the dutiful son, the unappreciated husband, the conscientious manager of an estate his ancestors had built. Unlike the Master, he really *has* been treated unfairly. But rather than fighting back or protesting his mistreatment he withdraws, brooding about it until the suppressed resentment corrodes him from within.

Not only does he endure contempt and persecution without resisting, but he *participates* in his own humiliation. Henry submits to the Master's endless demands for funds, but conceals them from everyone else but Mackellar, letting himself appear miserly. Worse, when the Master returns, Henry allows his brother to make him look selfish and ungracious without trying to defend himself or enlighten his father and wife of the true state of affairs — till at last the Master provokes him to violence and apparent fratricide.

From that moment the decay of Henry's character is steep and irreversible. He remains reactive, but the essential weakness of his character grows more obvious. He neglects his business. When his wife relinquishes her old love for the Master and begins to return her husband's affection, he rejects her in turn, and focuses on his son the same obsessive adoration which (Mackellar suggests) had been the original source of the Master's corruption. He has grown convinced that no ordinary methods can

DUTTON WAS SLOW OF THOUGHT AND, FOLLOWING THE MASTER'S DIRECTION, DUTIFULLY LAID HIS GUN UPON THE MUD, WHEREUPON THE MASTER MOVED WITH LIGHTNING SPEED.

defeat his brother. The Master here is Stevenson's incubus indeed, but one created in its victim's own mind. In the grip of this belief Henry is more helpless and powerless than ever to

defend himself, until like an animal that gnaws off its own leg to escape a trap, he resorts to flight and murder to free himself from his demon, and so destroys himself.

First a victim, Henry is now the persecutor. Yet he still can't act directly. Once he had the strength for fratricide. By the end, he no longer has the ability to carry it out himself, but has to rely on evasion and third parties to carry out the crime already lodged in his heart. The fulfillment of his wish destroys his body, as the wish itself had slowly destroyed his spirit.

did they get married? Are the feelings of either one ever reciprocated? How do their attitudes toward the Master affect their feelings for each other?

•Is Henry Durie justified in considering himself an innocent victim of his brother's persecution? Is he at all responsible for the things that happen, or not? Why?

•What is Mackellar's role in the story? How do his biases affect his account of the events? Do you agree with his judgment of the other characters?

•How do the major historical events going on during the novel affect the events of the story? Are

they important to the novel, or are they just colorful background details?

STUDY QUESTIONS

•Does this novel have a hero? A villain? If you asked the characters themselves, would their answers agree with yours? Why or why not?

• What does the Master of Ballantrae do that's so bad? How does he justify it? Are his excuses valid?

•Analyze the changes in the relationship between Henry Durie and his cousin Alison over the course of the novel. Why

About the Essayist:

Beth Nachison is an Assistant Professor in the History Department at Southern Connecticut State University, where she specializes in the history of early modern France. She holds a B.A. from Dartmouth College and an M.A. and Ph.D. from the University of Iowa.